A GIFT FOR:
....

FROM:
....

Editor: Emily Osborn
Art Director: Kevin Swanson
Design & Production: Dan Horton

BOK4359

ISBN: 978-1-59530-275-5

Printed and bound in China

FEB12

A GRANDPARENT'S *Legacy*

Your Life Story
in Your Own Words

THOMAS NELSON
Since 1798

GIFT BOOKS

CONTENTS

Introduction

As the years go by, we become more and more aware of what's really important in life. With every passing season, we are reminded that the love and traditions a family shares are treasures beyond value.

Lying within our memories are the personal stories behind those treasures. This book is intended to help you recall and reflect upon those memories and to share them with the ones you love. Open-ended questions will ask you to think about your childhood, special relationships, cherished traditions, personal triumphs and failures, sad partings, and joyous reunions—all the events big and small that have helped you to become the person you are today.

As you think about the questions in this book, don't be intimidated to put your thoughts and memories on paper. Writing is an exercise of discovery. You may recall a particular sight or sound from your childhood. You may remember something you thought you had forgotten. Maybe you will see a past event from a different perspective. You have much to share—and you may find that you learn something about yourself in the process.

How you choose to complete this book is up to you. You may follow it from beginning to end or in random order. You might complete your journaling in one week or over the course of several years. Whatever method you choose, one thing is certain: the memories and messages you record here will be a gift beyond value. May this gift draw you closer to your family as you share it, and may your family enjoy the words and wonder it holds for years to come.

Beginnings

GRANDPARENTS HOLD OUR TINY HANDS
FOR JUST A LITTLE WHILE . . .
BUT OUR HEARTS FOREVER.

Beginnings

....

What is the date and place of your birth?

_____

What is your full given name?

_____

_____

Who selected your name? *Why did they choose it?*

_____

_____

_____

_____

_____

Do you have a nickname or did you have one as a child?
How did you get it?

_____

_____

_____

_____

_____

_____

_____

What is your mother's full name and the date and place of her birth?

_____

_____

_____

What is your father's full name and the date and place of his birth?

_____

_____

_____

What are the names of your siblings and the dates and places of their birth?

_____

_____

_____

_____

_____

_____

_____

_____

_____

_____

Beginnings

What are the names of your maternal grandparents;
the dates and places of their birth?

_____

_____

_____

_____

_____

_____

_____

What are the names of your paternal grandparents;
the dates and places of their birth?

_____

_____

_____

_____

_____

_____

_____

_____

_____

What is your spouse's full name and the date and place
of his or her birth?

_____

_____

_____

_____

What are the names of your children and the dates and
places of their birth?

_____

_____

_____

_____

_____

_____

_____

_____

_____

_____

_____

_____

_____

_____

Beginnings

What are the names of your grandchildren?

Great-grandchildren?

What are the dates and places of their birth?

_____

_____

_____

_____

_____

_____

_____

_____

_____

_____

_____

_____

_____

_____

_____

_____

_____

_____

Where did your family live at the time of your birth
and during your early years?

_____

_____

_____

_____

_____

_____

_____

_____

What memories do you have of your family's home
and circumstances during that time?

_____

_____

_____

_____

_____

_____

_____

_____

Beginnings

....

What kind of work did your parents do?

_____

_____

_____

_____

What do you think was the most wonderful thing
about your mother?

_____

_____

_____

_____

_____

What do you think was the most wonderful thing
about your father?

_____

_____

_____

_____

_____

_____

What are your early memories of your grandparents?

_____

_____

_____

_____

_____

_____

_____

_____

_____

_____

_____

_____

_____

_____

Where did they live?

_____

_____

_____

_____

Beginnings

....

What were their homes and their circumstances like?

_____

_____

_____

_____

_____

_____

_____

_____

_____

_____

_____

_____

What kind of work did they do?

_____

_____

_____

_____

_____

_____

_____

Describe a favorite memory of a visit with
your grandparents.

_____

_____

_____

_____

_____

_____

_____

_____

_____

_____

_____

_____

_____

_____

_____

_____

_____

_____

_____

_____

_____

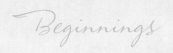
Beginnings

What memories or knowledge do you have of
your great-grandparents?

_____

_____

_____

_____

_____

_____

_____

_____

_____

_____

_____

_____

_____

_____

_____

_____

_____

_____

_____

_____

What do you know about your ancestors' origins?

_____

_____

_____

_____

_____

_____

_____

_____

_____

_____

_____

_____

_____

_____

_____

_____

_____

_____

_____

Childhood

TO BE A CHILD IS TO KNOW
THE JOY OF LIVING,
TO HAVE A CHILD IS TO KNOW
THE BEAUTY OF LIFE.

What are your earliest childhood memories?

_____

_____

_____

_____

_____

_____

_____

_____

_____

_____

_____

_____

_____

_____

_____

_____

_____

_____

_____

_____

Who among your childhood friends
do you remember now?

_____

_____

_____

_____

_____

_____

_____

_____

_____

_____

_____

_____

Are you still in contact with any of them?

_____

_____

_____

_____

_____

_____

Childhood

What did you and your family do for fun?

_____

_____

_____

_____

_____

_____

_____

_____

_____

_____

_____

_____

_____

_____

_____

_____

_____

_____

_____

_____

What were your other favorite pastimes as a child?

_____

_____

_____

_____

_____

_____

_____

_____

_____

_____

What was your favorite game or toy?

_____

_____

_____

_____

_____

_____

Did you ever have a hideaway, clubhouse, or other special place that was "yours"?

Describe this place.

_____

_____

_____

_____

_____

_____

_____

_____

_____

_____

_____

_____

_____

_____

_____

_____

_____

_____

What were some of your favorite store-bought treats as a child?

How much did they cost?

_____

_____

_____

_____

_____

_____

_____

_____

_____

_____

_____

_____

_____

_____

_____

_____

_____

_____

Childhood

What chores did you do as a child?

_____

_____

_____

_____

_____

_____

_____

_____

_____

Did you get an allowance? _How much was it?_

_____

_____

_____

_____

_____

_____

_____

_____

_____

_____

Describe the neighborhood you grew up in.

_____

_____

_____

_____

_____

_____

_____

_____

_____

_____

_____

_____

_____

_____

_____

_____

_____

_____

_____

Childhood

Did you have any pets?

What do you most remember about them?

_____

_____

_____

_____

_____

_____

_____

_____

_____

_____

_____

_____

_____

_____

_____

_____

_____

_____

_____

Were you part of a club, troop, or other organization as a child? *What do you remember about your group?*

_____

_____

_____

_____

_____

_____

_____

_____

_____

_____

_____

_____

_____

_____

_____

_____

_____

_____

_____

_____

Childhood

What mischievous childhood experience do you remember most?

_____

_____

_____

_____

_____

_____

_____

_____

_____

_____

_____

_____

_____

_____

_____

_____

_____

_____

_____

_____

What was the silliest thing you ever did as a child?

_____

_____

_____

_____

_____

_____

_____

_____

_____

_____

_____

_____

_____

_____

_____

_____

_____

_____

_____

_____

Childhood

What are the things you did in your childhood that
you are most glad you did?

_____

_____

_____

_____

_____

_____

_____

_____

What things do you wish you had done in childhood
or adolescence?

_____

_____

_____

_____

_____

_____

_____

_____

What did you want to be when you grew up?

How did that change over time?

_____

_____

_____

_____

_____

_____

_____

_____

_____

_____

_____

_____

_____

_____

_____

_____

_____

_____

_____

_____

Education

LEARNING IS A LIFETIME JOURNEY.
GROWING OLDER MERELY ADDS
EXPERIENCE TO KNOWLEDGE
AND WISDOM TO CURIOSITY.

Education

Where did you attend elementary school?

_____

_____

_____

Where did you attend middle school?

_____

_____

_____

Where did you attend high school?

_____

_____

_____

What are your earliest memories of attending school?

_____

_____

_____

_____

_____

_____

_____

_____

What did you enjoy most about school?

_____

_____

_____

_____

_____

_____

_____

What did you like least?

_____

_____

_____

_____

_____

_____

_____

_____

Education

How far did you have to travel to attend elementary
school and high school, and how did you travel to them?

_____

_____

_____

_____

What were your school lunches like?

_____

_____

_____

_____

_____

_____

_____

_____

Do you remember how much a school cafeteria lunch cost?

_____

_____

_____

_____

_____

_____

What were your favorite subjects in elementary school?

_____

_____

_____

_____

_____

In high school?

_____

_____

_____

_____

_____

_____

_____

Who was your all-time favorite teacher and why?

_____

_____

_____

_____

_____

_____

Education

What extracurricular activities were you involved in during high school?

_____

_____

_____

_____

_____

_____

_____

_____

Why did you choose those activities?

_____

_____

_____

Which did you most enjoy? *Why?*

_____

_____

_____

_____

What other special interests did you have?

_____

_____

_____

_____

_____

_____

_____

_____

_____

Did you receive any awards or any special recognition
during your school years?

_____

_____

_____

_____

_____

_____

_____

_____

_____

Did you attend dances and parties?

What were they like?

_____

_____

_____

_____

_____

_____

_____

_____

_____

_____

_____

_____

_____

_____

_____

_____

_____

_____

_____

_____

_____

What kind of music did you and your friends listen to?

_____

_____

_____

_____

_____

_____

_____

_____

_____

What were some of your favorite bands, singers, and songs?

_____

_____

_____

_____

_____

_____

_____

_____

_____

Education

Who were the celebrities that teens admired then?

_____

_____

_____

_____

_____

_____

_____

_____

_____

_____

_____

_____

_____

_____

_____

_____

_____

_____

_____

_____

What movies are memorable from that time?

_____

_____

_____

_____

_____

_____

_____

_____

_____

_____

_____

_____

_____

_____

_____

_____

_____

_____

_____

_____

Education

What fashion trends do you remember from high school?

_____

_____

_____

_____

_____

_____

_____

_____

Did you follow them? *Why or why not?*

_____

_____

_____

_____

_____

_____

_____

_____

_____

How did you and your friends behave or dress that concerned your parents?

_____

_____

_____

_____

_____

_____

_____

_____

_____

_____

_____

_____

_____

_____

_____

_____

_____

_____

Did you have a car in high school? What kind?

Were you proud of it?

_____

_____

_____

_____

_____

If you could have had any kind of car you wanted then, what would it have been and why?

_____

_____

_____

_____

_____

What kinds of cars did your family have then?

Were you proud of them or embarrassed by them?

_____

_____

_____

_____

_____

How did you learn to drive?

Education

What were your goals and aspirations after high school?

How did these change with time?

_____

_____

_____

_____

_____

_____

_____

_____

_____

_____

_____

_____

_____

_____

_____

_____

_____

_____

_____

_____

_____

_____

Did you continue your studies? *If so, where?*

_____

_____

_____

_____

_____

_____

_____

_____

_____

_____

_____

_____

_____

_____

_____

_____

_____

_____

Did you move away from home? *If so, describe this experience.*

_____

_____

_____

_____

_____

_____

_____

_____

What was your first place like?

_____

_____

_____

_____

_____

_____

_____

_____

_____

_____

What are some of your favorite memories from
the years following high school?

_____

_____

_____

_____

_____

_____

_____

_____

_____

_____

_____

_____

_____

_____

_____

_____

_____

_____

_____

_____

_____

_____

Career

THERE IS NO ONE ROAD TO SUCCESS.
THERE ARE AS MANY
AS THERE ARE PEOPLE
WILLING TO BUILD THEM.

Career

What did you want to be when you grew up?

_____

_____

_____

_____

_____

_____

Did you babysit or do other kinds of work for money
when you were young?

_____

_____

_____

_____

_____

Do you remember how much you were paid?

_____

_____

_____

_____

_____

What did you learn from those experiences?

_____

_____

_____

_____

_____

_____

_____

_____

_____

What was your first job following your education?

How did you get it?

_____

_____

_____

_____

_____

_____

_____

_____

Career

What did you enjoy about your work?

_____

_____

_____

_____

_____

_____

_____

_____

Have there been any particular challenges?

_____

_____

_____

_____

_____

_____

_____

_____

What was the most rewarding job you ever had?

_____

_____

_____

_____

_____

_____

_____

_____

_____

What was the worst job you ever had?

_____

_____

_____

_____

_____

_____

_____

_____

_____

Career

Has a career or job ever required you to move?

Where did you go and how did you feel about it?

_____

_____

_____

_____

_____

_____

_____

_____

_____

_____

_____

_____

_____

_____

_____

_____

_____

_____

Have any of your jobs involved travel?

Describe a memorable trip.

_____

_____

_____

_____

_____

_____

_____

_____

_____

_____

_____

_____

_____

_____

_____

_____

_____

_____

_____

_____

Career

Has anyone ever acted as a mentor to you?

_____

_____

_____

_____

_____

_____

_____

_____

_____

_____

_____

_____

_____

_____

_____

_____

_____

_____

_____

_____

What special friends have you made as a result of your work?

_____

_____

_____

_____

_____

_____

_____

_____

_____

_____

_____

_____

_____

_____

_____

_____

_____

_____

_____

Love &
Marriage

TWO HEARTS THAT SHARE
ONE LOVE, ONE LIFE
SO OFTEN KNOW TRUE JOY.

Love & Marriage

Who was your first crush?

_____

_____

_____

_____

_____

When did you attend your first boy/girl party?

_____

_____

_____

_____

_____

What do you remember about your first kiss?

_____

_____

_____

_____

_____

_____

What do you remember about your first date?

_____

_____

_____

_____

_____

_____

_____

_____

_____

What was a typical date like at that time?

_____

_____

_____

_____

_____

_____

_____

_____

_____

Who was your first love? How did you meet?

_____

_____

_____

_____

_____

_____

_____

_____

_____

What did you learn from that or other early
romantic relationships?

_____

_____

_____

_____

_____

_____

_____

_____

_____

How old were you when you met your spouse?

_____

_____

_____

_____

_____

_____

_____

_____

How did you meet?

_____

_____

_____

_____

_____

_____

_____

_____

_____

_____

What attracted you to your spouse?

_____

_____

_____

_____

_____

_____

_____

_____

What was your first impression of him or her?

_____

_____

_____

_____

_____

_____

_____

_____

_____

_____

What kinds of things did you enjoy doing together?

_____

_____

_____

_____

_____

_____

_____

Share a memory from when you were dating.

_____

_____

_____

_____

_____

_____

_____

_____

_____

When did you know that your spouse was "the one"?

_____

_____

_____

_____

_____

_____

_____

_____

_____

_____

_____

_____

_____

_____

_____

_____

_____

_____

_____

_____

Describe the marriage proposal.

_____

_____

_____

_____

_____

_____

_____

_____

_____

_____

_____

_____

_____

_____

_____

_____

_____

_____

Where and when were you married?

_____

_____

_____

_____

_____

_____

How many guests attended the wedding?

_____

_____

_____

_____

_____

Did you have a wedding song?

_____

_____

_____

_____

_____

_____

What is your most cherished memory from
your wedding day?

_____

_____

_____

_____

_____

_____

_____

_____

_____

_____

_____

_____

_____

_____

_____

_____

_____

_____

_____

What did you wear?

_____

_____

_____

_____

_____

_____

_____

_____

_____

What did your spouse wear?

_____

_____

_____

_____

_____

_____

_____

_____

_____

Is there a particularly special moment that you recall?

_____

_____

_____

_____

_____

_____

_____

_____

_____

_____

_____

_____

_____

_____

_____

_____

_____

_____

_____

_____

Where did you go on your honeymoon?

_____

_____

_____

_____

_____

_____

_____

_____

_____

_____

_____

_____

_____

_____

_____

_____

_____

_____

_____

_____

_____

What was your first home together like?

_____

_____

_____

_____

_____

_____

_____

_____

_____

_____

_____

_____

_____

_____

_____

_____

_____

_____

_____

_____

Has there been an anniversary celebration
that was extra special?

_____
_____
_____
_____
_____
_____
_____
_____
_____
_____
_____
_____
_____
_____
_____
_____
_____
_____
_____
_____
_____
_____

What did you love best about your mate
as your relationship matured?

_____

_____

_____

_____

_____

_____

_____

_____

What leisure and social activities have you
most enjoyed together?

_____

_____

_____

_____

_____

_____

_____

_____

What have been the most rewarding aspects
of your marriage?

_____

_____

_____

_____

_____

_____

_____

_____

_____

_____

_____

_____

_____

_____

_____

_____

_____

_____

_____

_____

Parenting

TO BE A PARENT IS TO SEE
THROUGH THE EYES OF LOVE
AND LISTEN WITH THE HEART.

What was your reaction when you found out you were going to be a parent?

_____

_____

_____

_____

_____

_____

_____

_____

_____

_____

_____

_____

_____

_____

_____

_____

_____

_____

_____

_____

_____

Where did you live when your first child was born?

_____

_____

_____

_____

What were your circumstances at that time?

_____

_____

_____

_____

_____

_____

_____

_____

_____

_____

_____

_____

_____

Parenting

What is your most vivid memory of being a new parent?

_____

_____

_____

_____

_____

_____

_____

_____

_____

_____

_____

_____

_____

_____

_____

_____

_____

_____

_____

_____

What did you enjoy most about it?

_____

_____

_____

_____

_____

_____

_____

_____

_____

What was most difficult for you?

_____

_____

_____

_____

_____

_____

_____

_____

_____

Parenting

What similarities with your mother do you now see
in yourself or in your children?

_____

_____

_____

_____

_____

_____

_____

What similarities with your father do you now see
in yourself or in your children?

_____

_____

_____

_____

_____

_____

_____

_____

What similarities do you see among your children
and your grandchildren?

_____

_____

_____

_____

_____

_____

_____

_____

_____

_____

_____

_____

_____

_____

_____

_____

_____

_____

Parenting

What was your greatest joy in being a parent?

_____

_____

_____

_____

_____

_____

_____

_____

What was your greatest challenge?

_____

_____

_____

_____

_____

_____

_____

_____

_____

_____

What values did you nurture in your children?

_____

_____

_____

_____

_____

_____

_____

_____

_____

_____

_____

_____

_____

_____

_____

_____

_____

_____

_____

Parenting

What was difficult for you to deal with during your children's school years?

_____

_____

_____

_____

_____

_____

_____

_____

_____

_____

_____

_____

_____

_____

_____

_____

_____

_____

_____

_____

_____

How have your children made you proud?

_____

_____

_____

_____

_____

_____

_____

_____

_____

_____

_____

_____

_____

_____

_____

_____

_____

_____

_____

_____

Parenting

What was it like to have your children, especially the first child, move away from home?

_____

_____

_____

_____

_____

_____

_____

_____

_____

_____

_____

_____

_____

_____

_____

_____

_____

_____

_____

What family traditions have you enjoyed passing to
your children and grandchildren?

_____

_____

_____

_____

_____

_____

_____

_____

_____

_____

_____

_____

_____

_____

_____

_____

_____

_____

_____

_____

Parenting

What are the things you hope your children
learned from you?

_____

_____

_____

_____

_____

_____

_____

_____

_____

_____

_____

_____

_____

_____

_____

_____

_____

What is the most important thing you learned
from being a parent?

_____

_____

_____

_____

_____

_____

_____

_____

_____

_____

_____

_____

_____

_____

_____

_____

_____

_____

_____

At Home

HOME IS WHERE FRIENDS AND FAMILY
MAKE EACH MOMENT MORE MEANINGFUL
AND EACH DAY A LITTLE BRIGHTER.

When and where did you buy your first home?

_____

_____

_____

_____

_____

Describe the house and its significance for you.

_____

_____

_____

_____

_____

_____

_____

_____

_____

_____

_____

_____

_____

What other houses have you lived in as an adult?

_____

_____

_____

_____

_____

_____

_____

_____

_____

Which did you like most and why?

_____

_____

_____

_____

_____

_____

_____

_____

What would have been a typical daily routine for you
when your children were in school?

_____

_____

_____

_____

_____

_____

_____

_____

_____

_____

_____

_____

_____

_____

_____

_____

_____

_____

What chores were your children responsible for?

_____

_____

_____

_____

_____

_____

_____

_____

Were they given an allowance? *If so, how much?*

_____

_____

_____

_____

_____

_____

_____

_____

_____

_____

What was a typical weeknight dinner during your children's school years?

_____

_____

_____

_____

_____

_____

_____

_____

What meal was a family favorite?

_____

_____

_____

_____

_____

_____

_____

_____

_____

_____

Did you eat out? Did you have a favorite place to go?

_____

_____

_____

_____

_____

_____

_____

_____

_____

Did you have a favorite dish in particular that
you liked to order?

_____

_____

_____

_____

_____

_____

_____

_____

What snacks and special treats did the family enjoy?

_____

_____

_____

_____

_____

_____

_____

_____

_____

_____

_____

_____

_____

_____

_____

_____

_____

_____

_____

_____

_____

_____

What was an extra-special fun thing for the
family to do together?

_____

_____

_____

_____

_____

_____

_____

_____

_____

_____

_____

_____

_____

_____

_____

_____

_____

_____

Describe your first family car.

_____

_____

_____

_____

_____

Were you proud of it?

_____

_____

_____

How did you acquire it, and how much did it cost?

_____

_____

_____

_____

_____

_____

_____

How much did gas cost at that time?

_____

_____

What other cars have you owned?

_____

_____

_____

_____

_____

_____

_____

_____

Was there one that particularly fit your personality?

_____

_____

_____

What made it fit so well?

_____

_____

_____

_____

_____

_____

Leisure

FAMILY TIMES TOGETHER,
        WHETHER QUIET AND THOUGHTFUL
OR FILLED WITH FUN AND LAUGHTER,
        ARE THE TIMES THAT MEAN THE MOST.

Leisure

What games and activities did your family enjoy
when you were a child?

_____

_____

_____

_____

_____

_____

_____

_____

_____

_____

_____

_____

_____

_____

_____

_____

_____

_____

_____

_____

Did you share any of these games with your children?

_____

_____

_____

_____

_____

_____

_____

_____

_____

_____

_____

_____

_____

_____

_____

_____

_____

_____

Leisure

How did you fill your childhood summer days?

_____

_____

_____

_____

_____

_____

_____

_____

How did your children fill theirs?

_____

_____

_____

_____

_____

_____

_____

_____

Share a family memory or tradition from
the Fourth of July.

_____

_____

_____

_____

_____

_____

_____

_____

_____

_____

_____

_____

_____

_____

_____

_____

_____

_____

Leisure

Please recall a driving trip you took with your parents
when you were young.

_____

_____

_____

_____

_____

_____

_____

_____

_____

_____

_____

_____

_____

_____

_____

_____

_____

_____

_____

_____

_____

Now recall a driving trip with your children.

_____

_____

_____

_____

_____

_____

_____

_____

_____

_____

_____

_____

_____

_____

_____

_____

_____

_____

_____

_____

_____

Leisure

What books and movies do you remember from
your childhood?

_____

_____

_____

_____

_____

_____

_____

_____

_____

_____

_____

_____

_____

_____

_____

_____

_____

_____

_____

What books and movies did your children most enjoy?

_____

_____

_____

_____

_____

_____

_____

_____

_____

_____

_____

_____

_____

_____

_____

_____

_____

_____

_____

Leisure

Who were your best friends after you were married?

_____

_____

_____

_____

_____

_____

_____

_____

_____

What did you enjoy most about the friendships?

_____

_____

_____

_____

_____

_____

_____

_____

_____

What social activities have you most enjoyed as an adult?

_____

_____

_____

_____

_____

_____

_____

_____

_____

_____

_____

_____

_____

_____

_____

_____

_____

_____

_____

_____

Leisure

What did you do for child-free entertainment when
your children were young?

_____

_____

_____

_____

_____

_____

_____

_____

_____

_____

_____

_____

_____

_____

_____

_____

_____

_____

_____

What did your family do on evenings and weekends for fun?

_____

_____

_____

_____

_____

_____

_____

_____

_____

_____

_____

_____

_____

_____

_____

_____

_____

_____

_____

_____

Leisure

What family gatherings have been most memorable?

_____

_____

_____

_____

_____

_____

_____

_____

_____

_____

_____

_____

_____

_____

_____

_____

_____

_____

_____

_____

_____

Did you visit your grandparents? Did they visit you?

What did you like or dislike about those visits?

_____

_____

_____

_____

_____

_____

_____

_____

_____

_____

_____

_____

_____

_____

_____

_____

_____

_____

_____

_____

Leisure

What was the first trip you ever took by plane? *How old were you? How did you feel about it?*

_____

_____

_____

_____

_____

_____

_____

What was the first trip you ever took alone?
Do you remember feeling nervous? Confident?

_____

_____

_____

_____

_____

_____

_____

What have been some of your favorite vacations?

_____

_____

_____

_____

_____

_____

_____

_____

_____

_____

_____

_____

_____

_____

_____

_____

_____

_____

_____

Leisure

What is the most fascinating place you've visited?

_____

_____

_____

_____

_____

_____

_____

_____

What places would you still like to visit? *Why?*

_____

_____

_____

_____

_____

_____

_____

_____

_____

_____

What was the most significant event you ever attended?

Why was it important to you?

_____

_____

_____

_____

_____

_____

_____

_____

_____

_____

_____

_____

_____

_____

_____

_____

_____

_____

_____

_____

_____

Celebrations

FAMILY TRADITIONS STAY WITH US
THROUGH TIME AND CHANGE,
LIKE PRECIOUS ORNAMENTS
BROUGHT OUT FROM YEAR TO YEAR.

Celebrations

How did your family celebrate special occasions when you were a child?

With a party, family, and friends or quietly at home?

_____

_____

_____

_____

_____

_____

_____

_____

_____

_____

_____

_____

_____

_____

_____

_____

_____

How was your birthday celebrated when you were young?

_____

_____

_____

_____

_____

_____

_____

_____

_____

_____

_____

_____

_____

_____

_____

_____

_____

_____

Celebrations

What was the most special birthday gift you ever received?

_____

_____

_____

_____

_____

_____

_____

_____

_____

_____

_____

_____

_____

_____

_____

_____

_____

_____

_____

_____

How did you celebrate your children's birthdays?

_____

_____

_____

_____

_____

_____

_____

_____

_____

_____

_____

_____

_____

_____

_____

_____

_____

_____

_____

Celebrations

....

What is your favorite memory of a birthday celebration?

_____

_____

_____

_____

_____

_____

_____

_____

_____

_____

_____

_____

_____

_____

_____

_____

_____

_____

_____

_____

What holiday traditions from your childhood
did you pass on to your children?

_____

_____

_____

_____

_____

_____

_____

_____

_____

_____

_____

_____

_____

_____

_____

_____

_____

_____

_____

_____

Celebrations

Did you begin any new traditions with your children?

_____

_____

_____

_____

_____

_____

_____

_____

_____

_____

_____

_____

_____

_____

_____

_____

_____

_____

_____

_____

_____

_____

Do your children continue those traditions
with your grandchildren?

_____

_____

_____

_____

_____

_____

_____

_____

_____

_____

_____

_____

_____

_____

_____

_____

_____

_____

_____

Celebrations

What holiday celebrations from your childhood stand out most in your memory?

_____

_____

_____

_____

_____

_____

_____

_____

_____

_____

_____

_____

_____

_____

_____

_____

_____

_____

_____

_____

What was a favorite holiday food in your childhood days?

_____

_____

_____

_____

_____

_____

_____

What family recipe have you passed on to your children
and hope that they will pass on to your grandchildren?

_____

_____

_____

_____

_____

_____

_____

_____

_____

Celebrations

What holiday have your children most enjoyed celebrating?

_____

_____

_____

_____

_____

_____

_____

_____

_____

_____

_____

_____

_____

_____

_____

_____

_____

_____

_____

_____

_____

What has been the most meaningful holiday for you
as a parent and a grandparent?

_____

_____

_____

_____

_____

_____

_____

_____

_____

_____

_____

_____

_____

_____

_____

_____

_____

_____

_____

Life Events

NO TRUTH TAUGHT BY OTHERS GIVES US
STRENGTH AS GREAT AS THAT WHICH WE CAN
FIND WITHIN OUR OWN EXPERIENCES.

What were your feelings when your first child got married?

_____

_____

_____

_____

_____

_____

_____

_____

_____

_____

_____

_____

_____

_____

_____

_____

_____

_____

_____

_____

_____

_____

_____

Describe your reaction to the birth of your first grandchild.

What other family events have been
of special importance to you?

_____

_____

_____

_____

_____

_____

_____

_____

_____

_____

_____

_____

_____

_____

_____

_____

_____

_____

_____

_____

_____

Have you or other family members served in the military?

_____

_____

_____

_____

_____

_____

_____

_____

_____

_____

_____

_____

_____

_____

_____

_____

_____

_____

_____

Life Events

Have you ever been in an accident, had major
surgery, or suffered a similar challenge?

_____

_____

_____

_____

_____

_____

_____

_____

_____

_____

_____

_____

_____

_____

_____

_____

_____

_____

_____

_____

_____

Did tragedy ever strike you or a loved one?

If so, how did your family and friends respond?

_____

_____

_____

_____

_____

_____

_____

_____

_____

_____

_____

_____

_____

_____

_____

_____

_____

_____

_____

_____

_____

_____

Life Events

What is the most difficult choice you ever had to make?

Would you make the same decision again?

_____

_____

_____

_____

_____

_____

_____

_____

_____

_____

_____

_____

_____

_____

_____

_____

_____

_____

_____

_____

What do you see as the most important political
or international events of your lifetime?

_____

_____

_____

_____

_____

_____

_____

_____

_____

_____

_____

_____

_____

_____

_____

_____

_____

_____

_____

Have you ever actively participated in politics or in a rally
or a demonstration? What was the cause?

What did you think of the experience?

_____

_____

_____

_____

_____

_____

_____

_____

_____

_____

_____

_____

_____

_____

_____

_____

_____

_____

What do you regard as the most important invention
of your lifetime? *How did it affect you?*

_____

_____

_____

_____

_____

_____

_____

_____

_____

_____

_____

_____

_____

_____

_____

_____

_____

_____

_____

_____

_____

What has been your greatest reward in life?

_____

_____

_____

_____

_____

_____

_____

_____

_____

_____

_____

_____

_____

_____

_____

_____

_____

_____

_____

_____

_____

_____

What have been life's most difficult challenges?

Life Events

What was the happiest time of your life?

_____

_____

_____

_____

_____

_____

_____

_____

_____

What was the saddest?

_____

_____

_____

_____

_____

_____

_____

_____

_____

What was the busiest time of your life?

_____

_____

_____

_____

_____

_____

_____

_____

_____

What was the most relaxed?

_____

_____

_____

_____

_____

_____

_____

_____

_____

Inspiration

SOME GIFTS YOU HOLD
IN YOUR HAND...
SOME YOU HOLD
IN YOUR HEART.

What role does religion or spirituality play
in your life? *Has it changed over the years?*

_____

_____

_____

_____

_____

_____

_____

_____

_____

_____

_____

_____

_____

_____

_____

_____

_____

_____

_____

_____

Who has made the greatest impact on your life?

_____

_____

_____

_____

_____

_____

_____

_____

_____

_____

_____

_____

_____

_____

_____

_____

_____

_____

_____

_____

_____

_____

Inspiration

Who were your role models when you were young?

_____

_____

_____

_____

_____

_____

_____

_____

_____

_____

_____

_____

_____

_____

_____

_____

_____

_____

_____

What valuable advice did you receive when you were young?

_____

_____

_____

_____

_____

_____

_____

_____

_____

_____

_____

_____

_____

_____

_____

_____

_____

_____

_____

Who have you consulted most often for guidance over the years?

_____

_____

_____

_____

_____

_____

_____

_____

_____

_____

_____

_____

_____

_____

_____

_____

_____

_____

_____

Who do you turn to now for advice?

Is there a certain place that you go to for comfort
or to unwind? *Why is this place meaningful?*

_____

_____

_____

_____

_____

_____

_____

_____

_____

_____

_____

_____

_____

_____

_____

_____

_____

_____

_____

_____

What advice would you give future generations of your family?

_____

_____

_____

_____

_____

_____

_____

_____

_____

_____

_____

_____

_____

_____

_____

_____

_____

_____

_____

_____

What are your most treasured possessions?

Why are they of special value?

_____

_____

_____

_____

_____

_____

_____

_____

_____

_____

_____

_____

_____

_____

_____

_____

_____

_____

_____

_____

_____

_____

If you could keep only one family photo,
which would it be? *Why?*

_____

_____

_____

_____

_____

_____

_____

_____

_____

_____

_____

_____

_____

_____

_____

_____

_____

_____

_____

What is the most important lesson you've
learned about life?

_____

_____

_____

_____

_____

_____

_____

_____

_____

_____

_____

_____

_____

_____

_____

_____

_____

_____

_____

Inspiration

What do you consider to be life's greatest gifts?

_____

_____

_____

_____

_____

_____

_____

_____

_____

_____

_____

_____

_____

_____

_____

_____

_____

_____

_____

_____

Inspiration

How would you describe success?

_____

_____

_____

_____

_____

_____

_____

_____

_____

What do you feel is one way to achieve it?

_____

_____

_____

_____

_____

_____

_____

_____

_____

What are your hopes for your family over the next ten years?

Please record any other favorite memories.

_____

_____

_____

_____

_____

_____

_____

_____

_____

_____

_____

_____

_____

_____

_____

_____

_____

_____

_____

_____

Inspiration

Inspiration

Inspiration

WE'D LOVE TO HEAR
IF YOU HAVE ENJOYED USING
AND SHARING THIS BOOK.

....

Please send your comments to:
Hallmark Book Feedback
P.O. Box 419034
Mail Drop 215
Kansas City, MO 64141
Or e-mail us at:
booknotes@hallmark.com